Make Your Will

First published in 2009 by
Liberties Press
Guinness Enterprise Centre | Taylor's Lane | Dublin 8
Tel: +353 (1) 415 1286
www.LibertiesPress.com | info@libertiespress.com

Distributed in the United States by
Dufour Editions | PO Box 7 | Chester Springs | Pennsylvania 19425

and in Australia by
InBooks | 3 Narabang Way | Belrose NSW 2085

Trade enquiries to CMD BookSource
55A Spruce Avenue | Stillorgan Industrial Park
Blackrock | County Dublin
Tel: +353 (1) 294 2560 | Fax: +353 (1) 294 2564

Copyright © John G. Murphy, Jason Dunne and Michael Freeman, 2009

The authors have asserted their moral rights.

ISBN: 978–1–905483–59–4
2 4 6 8 10 9 7 5 3 1

A CIP record for this title is available from the British Library.

Editing by Michael Freeman and Liberties Press
Cover design by Ros Murphy
Internal design by Liberties Press
Printed in Ireland by Colour Books | 105 Baldoyle Industrial Estate | Dublin 13

Make Your Will

The Irish Guide to Putting
Your Affairs in Order

John G. Murphy

and Jason Dunne

LIB ERT IES

Dedicated to the memory of Nuala O'Faolain,
author and journalist, whose last will and testament
should be an inspiration to us all

Disclaimer

Every effort has been made to ensure that the information provided in this book is both accurate and up to date. If you notice any errors or omissions, we would appreciate if you would let us know as soon as possible. The information provided is of a general nature. The publishers and authors and their servants or agents assume no responsibility for and give no guarantees, undertakings or warranties concerning the accuracy, completeness or up-to-date nature of the information provided in this publication at this time and do not accept any liability whatsoever arising from any errors or omissions. If you need advice, consult with a trusted qualified adviser.

Contents

Acknowledgements

Seán O'Keeffe and Peter O'Connell of Liberties Press inspired us to write this book. They not alone inspired, but also cajoled, pushed, pulled and guided us until we researched, wrote and edited several drafts. Then they gave our raw copy to their brilliant team of subeditors, proofreaders and designers, Orlaith Delaney, Dan Bolger, Caroline Lambe and Ros Murphy. We thank them for transforming the copy into this book.

They did likewise for the production of our book *Inheritance and Succession: The Complete Irish Guide* and helped it become a national best-seller, with reviews on TV and radio, and in newspapers and magazines throughout the country and abroad.

To produce *Make Your Will*, we drew upon a wealth of talent and support from a great many sources, including our colleagues at John A. Sinnott & Co, Solicitors, where there is a collective experience of about one hundred years of assisting people with their wills. We thank them.

Louise Murphy, Siobhan Dunne and Brigid Freeman had tremendous patience and gave us steadfast support during our months of research, editing and writing of this book. A very special, personal thanks to them.

We salute the many people who have already made their wills, and we encourage the many who have not already done so, to do it.

JOHN G. MURPHY, JASON DUNNE AND MICHAEL FREEMAN

Introduction

It is a shocking fact that half of those of us who are eligible have not made a will. This is not surprising. Up to now, the making of a will has been an obstacle course.

One obstacle has been the challenge of 'going to see the solicitor'. This was a daunting task that people did perhaps only twice in their lives: once when they bought their house, and for a second time when they made their will. Today, going to the solicitor should be as easy as going to the supermarket. As a rule of thumb, people should review their wills every few years, or when their personal circumstances change.

Another obstacle to making a will was deciding what to do with your estate and how best to care for your loved ones after you die. With the help of a good solicitor and some careful planning, that process can be made easy. Yet another obstacle is the notion that you are tempting fate and will die if you make a will. We assure you that you will not die as a result of making your will!

Many people decide to avoid making a will as they believe that it makes no difference whether they have a will or not. As solicitors of many years' experience, we urge them to make a will and, even if they have little in the way of material possessions, at least to leave a legacy of good memories.

This book sets out to enable everyone to make a will or, if they have made one already, to update it. It will show why wills are important, the factors to consider in the process of making your will, and what happens if you don't make a will. It will help people to decide on what to do with their estate, put aside their worries about will-making, demystify the process, and avoid creating stress and worry for their relations.

If you are thinking of making your will, turn it into a positive step. Seize the moment, do it, and then get on with living. You can rest easy in the knowledge that your affairs are in order.

1

It's All About Life

The funny thing about writing a will is that it is less about death and more about life. At some stage, we will all check out, go to the lonesome valley or, in other words, die.

But don't dwell on that. Let's get some clarity on how to live life better while we're here. Let's squeeze as much joy as we can out of each day. And if we can, let's clear our conscience and make the life of another family member, or that of someone else, better too.

If you have loved ones, they will feel terribly sad and will grieve when you are gone. You can spare them a lot of sadness and trauma if you make a will. By making a will, you have the power to prevent potential conflict and avoid costly court cases.

If you die without making a will, your chance will be gone. Of course, you may wish to exclude someone from your estate. But by making a will, *you* get to decide on what happens. If you leave no will, someone whom you may not want to receive anything from your estate may get a share of it. This may be a sibling you haven't spoken to for years. In extreme cases, the State may get your property if no other relative can be found.

Some won't make a will at all. In other words, they will die intestate. This frequently leaves a legacy of bitterness and creates a legal nightmare that may last for many years or even generations.

When you make your will, you create a legal document in which you decide who is going to inherit your estate when you die. Through your will, you may make someone richer or you may make provision for the protection of someone you love dearly. You may of course create disappointment for someone else. You can't please everyone. However, as you will find out in this book, the advantages of having a will far outweigh the disadvantages of not having one.

The process of writing a will always intrigues people. It forces most people to stop and take stock, and to think about what they have or do not have. Some are surprised to discover that they have more than they thought they did. Others obtain complete clarification about what they have and who they would like to leave it to.

The authors, experienced solicitors, urge you to make a will. It's in your interest.

The Eldest Son

The eldest son was the heir apparent. He inherited the property as if this was the orderly thing to do. The reason was that he was 'destined' to be the next provider for the family. The property passed down, from generation to generation, to the eldest son each time.

Two daughters could inherit the property jointly if there was no son. Two women were deemed the same in law as one man. However, if there was only one daughter, she could not inherit.

That understanding prevailed only a generation ago. Thankfully, society has moved on. Subject only to a few restrictions, people in the Ireland of today make their wills and leave their property to whomsoever they wish.

2

Making a Will in Five Steps

If you haven't made a will before, or if you have already made one but have forgotten the content of it, here is a simple approach in five steps:

1. On a sheet of paper, write out a list of all the things you own, e.g. your house, your car, your CD collection, and so on. This is called your *estate*.

2. Choose two people whom you trust with your life. They will be your *executors*.

3. Write a list of the people you want to leave something to. They're called your *beneficiaries*.

4. Take a few sheets of paper and write a rough outline of your will.

5. Get two witnesses. Their job is to see you sign your name. They must sign below your signature on your will.

That's the procedure, and the framework for a will. However, there's a lot more to be considered.

3

Making a Will in One Step

The best way to start making your will is in one step. That step is simply to pick up the phone and make an appointment with your solicitor, who is an expert in will-making. Get your solicitor to work through it with you.

Even if you are a lawyer yourself, it is best to get another lawyer to help you make your will. Remember the old adage: 'If you are your own lawyer, you have a fool for a client.'

We often meet executors or beneficiaries of people who have made DIY wills, or have bought a 'will pack' off the shelf in a bookshop, filled it in, and sent it off to be stored in a safe somewhere. Years pass. The person who makes the will dies. It is discovered that the will is a complete mess and the case ends up in court, sometimes costing the entire estate in lawyers' fees.

In short, if you want your family and friends to remember you fondly, and you want to leave a good legacy, ask your solicitor to help you make your will.

There is much more to making a will than first meets the eye. Your estate, your age, your state of mind, the number of beneficiaries you have, your executors, and various tax issues are some of the relevant elements.

In the process of drawing up your will, you may learn some other things, such as how to avoid or reduce tax, how to put an enduring power of attorney in place, what to do about boundaries and neighbours, and so on, because all these things are likely to come up in a full discussion about you, your property and your wishes.

Think!

When going to meet with your solicitor, bring:

1. A list of your proposed beneficiaries. This is the list of family and friends to whom you wish to leave something from your estate

2. A list of your assets

3. The names of your executors and their addresses and contact details

4. Your personal affairs and possessions list (see Chapter 6).

These are the building blocks of your will. Working with your solicitor, you can create the first draft of your will from the above four building blocks.

Take the draft home with you, develop it and arrange a second meeting with your solicitor to finalise the draft and turn it into a valid and legal will.

4

Words for Wills:

Legal Language

Lawyers use words and phrases that are almost like a foreign language to most people. These are some of the terms they are likely to use when helping you to make a will:

WILL OR TESTAMENT A legal declaration of how a person wishes his or her possessions to be disposed of after their death.

CODICIL A document that amends or changes something in a will or some aspect of a will. Usually, it is best to make a new will. Codicils were made to avoid rewriting lengthy handwritten wills. Nowadays, because amendments can be made so easily on computer, codicils are less common.

TESTAMENTARY Of or relating to a will or testament, or bequeathed by a will or testament.

TESTATOR A man who makes a will.

TESTATRIX A woman who makes a will.

TO DIE TESTATE To die leaving a valid will.

To Die Intestate To die leaving no will or leaving a will that is invalid or does not deal with all your assets.

Revoke To cancel or render a will null and void.

Executor/Executrix A man or woman who is appointed by a testator to carry out the testator's will.

Administrator/Administratrix A man or woman appointed under the Succession Act or by a court to deal with a deceased person's property and affairs where the person died intestate.

Trustee A person (or institution) to whom legal title to property is entrusted to use for another's benefit. Legally, you must appoint two trustees. They are persons who will control and manage your property for the benefit of your chosen beneficiaries where the beneficiaries are in most cases either too young to manage it themselves or incapable, through mental or physical disability, of doing so. A trustee is different from an executor. If property is left to trustees, it is the executors' job to get the property to those trustees. The trustees then hold and manage the trust property until it is given to the beneficiaries.

Beneficiary A recipient of funds or other property under a will, trust, insurance policy, and so on.

Guardian A person who is entrusted by law with the care of the person and/or property of another person – a minor or someone who is legally incapable of managing his or her own affairs.

Testamentary Guardian A person appointed under a will to be a guardian of a child or children after the parent, who is the natural guardian, dies.

MINOR A person under eighteen years of age.

SPOUSE You may think this is obvious, but on occasion it is not. You must be legally and validly married to another person in order to be their spouse. There is no such thing as a 'common law spouse'.

BENEFIT A general term used to describe something that passes to a beneficiary under the terms of a will.

REAL PROPERTY Immovable property, such as land or a house.

PERSONAL PROPERTY Moveable property such as money, stock, shares, bonds and savings certificates.

DEVISE The word required in a will for passing real property (land or house) to a beneficiary.

DEVISEE The beneficiary who is to receive real property under your will.

BEQUEATH To leave something to a person in your will.

BEQUEST/LEGACY Something, usually personal property, that has been left to a person in your will.

RESIDUE The remainder of a person's property or assets not already specifically mentioned in their will.

RESIDUE CLAUSE A clause in a will to encompass all property not already specifically mentioned in the other parts of the will.

ISSUE Offspring, or children of offspring, of the deceased person.

AFFIDAVIT OF MENTAL CAPACITY A sworn document to verify that the testator/testatrix has, or had, the mental capacity to make the will at the time the will was made. It is usually completed by the solicitor who drafted the will or by one of the witnesses, or possibly by a doctor.

PROBATE/ADMINISTRATION These terms are used interchangeably to describe the process of dealing with the affairs of a deceased person. Probate applies where there is a will; administration where there is no will.

GRANT OF PROBATE The document issued by the High Court confirming that the will presented to the court officer is the deceased person's last will.

GRANT OF LETTERS OF ADMINISTRATION The document issued by the High Court to the next of kin to enable them to deal with the deceased person's estate, where there is no will.

CAVEAT A document lodged with the Probate Office to suspend a certain proceeding until the notifier has been given a hearing.

DISCLAIMER A document signed by a beneficiary who does not want to take a benefit left to them in a will. This is only relevant where the testator/testatrix has already died.

RENUNCIATION A document signed by a person, usually a spouse, who does not wish to receive any benefit under the other spouse's will, when they die. This must be signed during the lifetime of the other spouse.

MIRROR WILLS Where two people, typically a husband and wife, make identical wills, usually leaving their entire estates to each other.

COMMORIENTES (simultaneous death) Where two people die at the same time and it is impossible to determine which person died first (for instance, in a plane crash), they are both deemed to have died at exactly the same time.

GIFT OVER   This is an alternative-provision clause that is inserted into a will to cover unforeseen events, e.g. a beneficiary dying before the testator.

LEGAL-RIGHT SHARE   The share that a surviving spouse is entitled to in the deceased spouse's estate where the deceased spouse has not made adequate provision for the surviving spouse in their will. It applies only where the deceased died testate.

ENDURING POWER OF ATTORNEY   An enduring power of attorney (EPA) is a document you sign to allow your chosen attorney to deal with your assets if you become mentally incapacitated.

Think!

When you come to draw up your will, it is an opportune time to make an enduring power of attorney. To prepare an enduring power of attorney, you will need:

1. The name and contact details of your GP

2. The names and contact details of two notice parties

3. The names, addresses and contact details of two attorneys

4. The name, address and contact details of your bank, and details of your bank accounts.

5

Basic Elements of a Will

Building Blocks

Think about your will as being made up of a number of building blocks. To build your will, lay each block carefully. Keep it simple.

One of the building blocks of a good will is the Personal Affairs and Possessions List, given in this book. You can download a free, expandable version of the list from *www.myinheritance.ie.* You will find this list useful for focusing on what you have, and what you wish to do with your estate. If you lay this block first, you will be better prepared to meet your solicitor and so get more value from your meeting.

Discuss your wishes honestly and openly. This can lead to a useful analysis of your ideas for the will. An experienced solicitor will point out pitfalls and suggest solutions. The will should be tailored to your needs.

All wills must comply with the following requirements:

The Law

The Succession Act 1965 governs the formalities for making a valid will.

Your Age

You must be eighteen or over to make a will. There is no upper age limit. At one time, someone under eighteen could make a will if they were married: the legal age for marriage was sixteen. While you might think this un-likely, it used to happen. However, the Family Law Act 1995 (which became law in August 1996) increased the age limit for marriage from sixteen to eighteen.

Your Mind

You must be of 'sound disposing mind', which means that you must have the mental capacity to make a will. This is called 'testamentary capacity'. It includes being aware that you are making a will and disposing of prop-erty to other people on your death. You must also be aware of the extent of your possessions and property.

The solicitor usually assesses mental capacity when the will is made. If the solicitor knows the person al-ready, they should be aware of the person's mental ca-pacity. In most cases, it will be obvious that a person has the required capacity to make a will. When a will is made in a solicitor's office, it helps to establish that the person who made the will had the required capacity.

But in some cases the lines are not so clear-cut. Where the solicitor has a doubt as to the person's mental ca-pacity, it might be necessary to obtain a certificate from the person's doctor, stating that they are mentally able to make a will. If you lack the required capacity, you cannot make a will.

External factors, namely undue influence and duress, can also cause problems. In such a case, the person making the will comes under so much pressure that it influences their decisions. This pressure has many different forms, and ranges from emotional blackmail to threats or intimidation. Elderly, frail or ill people are more at risk of this, as they are more vulnerable. Unfortunately, 'elder abuse' is something that happens all too often, and solicitors have to be vigilant to spot it. In many cases, the person exerting the pressure over the elderly person may be a relative or someone close to them.

In Writing

The will must be in writing. (Pencil is unacceptable, as it can be erased.) A will can be handwritten but it must be clearly legible. Typed is better, as it is easier to read. Wills are usually written or typed on paper.

In two famous cases, wills that were not written on paper were admitted to probate as they complied with the formalities. One was a will written on an empty eggshell, and the other was a will written on the back of a car number plate. Both satisfied the requirements of the Probate Office and were admitted as validly made wills. Don't be tempted – use only paper!

Full Names and Addresses

The will should give the testator's full name and address. If you are known by any other name, or even a nickname, you should mention that name too. For example, if your name is Robert but are often known as Bob, you should give both names. Similarly, if you moved house recently, you should mention both your current and your former address.

A Revoking Clause

The will should contain a clause revoking any previous will you made. If you have made a will in a foreign country dealing with foreign assets, you must ensure that, in revoking your previous Irish will, you do not inadvertently revoke your foreign will too. Note that marriage revokes a will the moment you sign the marriage register. Divorce does not revoke a will.

Executors, Trustees and Guardians

Next, appoint executors. These are persons who will carry out your wishes when you die. You need only one executor, but it is wise to have two, just in case one dies, becomes mentally incapacitated or simply does not want to act. If necessary, you should appoint guardians and trustees. This is usually done in a case where there are young children or where there is a physically or mentally incapacitated child or adult. Trustees are needed to look after property where the beneficiary is unable to do so. Guardians look after the day-to-day activities of children, including contact with schools and teachers, and the trustees. The same people can act as executors, guardians and trustees if you wish.

Everything You Own

Next – and this is crucial – your will should dispose of absolutely everything you have or own. You might want to leave specific items to specific people. Some people simply leave everything to one person. One way or the other, be sure that your will covers all of your assets.

If you are giving everything to one person, you can say: 'I leave all my property to . . . ' If you are disposing of specific items to specific people, you should include a residue clause covering everything that has not been specified. The residue clause, which is usually inserted towards the end of the will, can prevent a partial intestacy arising.

A partial intestacy can arise if a beneficiary named in your will dies before you do. In this case, the gift to them will fail. Instead, it will be dealt with under the intestacy rules (see page 87) and will pass to your next of kin. If, however, you include a residue clause, the gift you left to that person will not fail but will instead pass to the residuary beneficiary named in your will.

There is a potential pitfall here. If a partial intestacy arises, people that you did not intend to benefit from your estate may in fact do so. In addition, the cost of administering your estate will be higher, as two different grants are required. One grant, the grant of probate, deals with the assets in your will, and the other, the grant of letters of administration intestate, deals with assets that fall outside your will.

Dated

Your will must be dated the day you sign it.

Signed

You must sign your will at the end. There are exceptions to this: at your direction, someone else can sign it. This may happen if you are blind or physically unable through disability to sign your own name. Alternatively, if a person cannot read or write, they can make a mark, such as an 'X', as their signature.

Witnessed

Two people must witness your signature. The witnesses need not know that they are witnessing a will; they are only witnessing your signature. The will can be covered with a sheet of paper to conceal its details, leaving only the space for the signatures of the testator/testatrix and witnesses visible.

Witnesses must be able to sign their own name; they cannot direct someone else to sign as a witness on their behalf. Because a witness must actually see you sign your name, a blind person cannot witness a will. The witnesses must make their signatures somewhere below your signature on the will.

The will should have a clause after or below the signature of the testator or testatrix, which records the fact that the testator or testatrix and the witnesses all witnessed in each other's presence.

The Succession Act 1965 does not state that the witnesses have to see each other sign. However, to eliminate any doubt, the clause at the end will usually record that all three people were present in the room at the same time and that they all witnessed each other sign. When the will has been signed and witnessed, nothing should be added, deleted or changed.

Gifts to Witnesses

A person who witnesses a will (or their spouse) cannot be a beneficiary under that will. Such gifts to witnesses are void. This safety net is built into the legislation to ensure that an unscrupulous person trying to cash in on the testator's property by exerting pressure on the testator is prohibited from receiving any benefit.

The solicitor and/or members of their staff usually witness wills. If you want to leave something to a particular person, just make sure they don't witness your will. An executor can also be a witness, provided of course that they are not also a beneficiary.

Documents Referred To in Your Will

If, in your will, you refer to a sealed envelope or a map, the envelope or map must already be in existence at the time your will is signed, and it must be stapled or clipped to the will prior to or at the time of signing. You cannot make the will and attach the map later.

Documents Referred To But Not Attached

If, for example, a map was attached at the time your will was made, but later became detached and lost, the will could end up in court. Use caution when attaching documents to a will or referring to documents in a will. Although solicitors are trained to deal with such situations, untold problems can arise if things go wrong.

That's it. These are the basic formalities for making a valid will. However, that is all they are: formalities. When it comes to drafting a will, following the formalities of the Succession Act is relatively straightforward. Problems arise when mistakes are made.

If It Goes Wrong

Many things can go wrong when using legal words, phrases and language, and for this reason alone you should always consult a solicitor when making your will. If your will goes wrong, it can go horribly wrong.

If your will is not valid, you will be deemed to have died intestate and your estate will be distributed amongst your next of kin. On the other hand, even if you leave a valid will, if you incorrectly name a beneficiary, the wrong person may end up benefiting from your will. When you die, it is too late to fix the mistake.

Think!

To decide on who your beneficiaries may be, consider the following:

- family members who have done a lot for you, will appreciate what you have done for them, will make the most of your estate and will carry on the family tradition

- a charity or church that you support

- friends who would benefit or appreciate what you have done

- someone who is experiencing hard times

- someone who is likely to do something for a son or daughter.

What proportion of your estate should you give to each one? How might you decide on the share you will give?

6

The Personal Affairs
and Possessions List

You may be amazed at what you have – and what you owe – when you think it out. Work through the following list as a guide and then complete the Personal Affairs and Possessions List (also downloadable from *www.myinheritance.ie*) that follows.

Assets

House and Land

Who holds the deeds of your house? If you have land, who has the deeds? Your deeds will usually be held by you, your bank, your building society or your solicitor. If you own your own home, on your death the mortgage will typically be cleared by the life policy which you would have taken out when you took out your mortgage. (Note: Deeds for land registry property will be abolished from 2010. See *www.landregistry.ie*.)

House Contents

If you are leaving your house and contents to one person, you don't really need to list the contents. If, however, you are leaving specific items to particular people, you need to describe these items clearly.

Investment Property

Do you own a house that you rent out? A holiday home? If so, where are the deeds? You should have a separate will for any foreign assets.

Interest in Expectancy

If your father leaves the family farm to your mother for her lifetime, and after her death it is left to you, you have an 'interest in expectancy'. Basically, you will be taking the farm from your father, but you will only get it when your mother dies.

Bank/Building Society Current/Deposit/ Savings Accounts

Keep deposit books in a safe place. If you close an account, and open a new one, or if you change banks, update your list.

Credit Union

In a credit union, you become a member, as opposed to a customer. If you have a loan outstanding when you die, the credit union is insured for the balance, provided that you were under seventy when you joined. The debt is usually repaid from the insurance.

Unlike with a bank or building society account, you can nominate the proceeds of the account to a person after your death. If you are unsure whether your account is nominated or not, you should contact your branch. The nominee you have chosen gets the credit union fund; it is not dealt with under your will.

Post Office

Do you have a Post Office account or saving bonds? Savings bonds are guaranteed by the State, and in the current uncertain economic climate, people are investing in secure financial products.

Prize Bonds

Do you have Prize Bonds? They are State-guaranteed and are entered into a draw every month. Where are the original bonds?

Cars, Boats, Motorcycles

Classic cars will appreciate in value over time. You may have a fishing boat or a motorcycle.

Stocks, Shares, Gold

Stocks and shares have been badly hit in recent times. But think of them as a long-term investment: in general, they will eventually recover in value. Whatever type of share or stock you have, be sure to keep the original certificates in a safe place and keep a record of them.

Pensions

Do you have a pension for your retirement, either private or State? Check the terms of it. Will it be payable only to you on your retirement, or will it be worth something on your death?

If you have been a net contributor all your life and have paid PAYE, you will be entitled to a contributory pension at age sixty-five.

ERS or EU retirement schemes are important to farmers: they facilitate early retirement from farming, usually at age fifty-five. Are you a member of such a scheme?

Life Insurance/Assurance

Do you have an insurance policy or an assurance policy? Some policies are payable on death; some are for a set term of years, after which you receive a lump sum.

For death cover only, you personally will get nothing. Tell your solicitor where the original life insurance and life assurance documents are located. Check to see if the proceeds of the policy (or policies) are nominated to anyone in the event of your death.

Antiques, Art, Wine, Heirlooms

Many families have heirlooms; these are sometimes worth nothing but in some cases can be surprisingly valuable. These include stamps, coins, and that All-Ireland medal!

Jewellery

Do you have diamonds, rubies, emeralds? An expensive watch or necklace? Something that has sentimental value to a member of your family? Make an inventory or list of your jewellery, especially if you have two items that are similar, and that you wish to leave to different people. This avoids confusion later. We have seen a major estate become embroiled in years of litigation due to a row over the silver spoons.

Cash

Despite recent well-publicised problems at the banks, don't resort to keeping cash under the proverbial mattress or in the biscuit tin.

Debts and Liabilities

Most people have debts or liabilities. If, like most of us, you have debts, manage them carefully, or they may take over and manage you. If you have debt worries, seek advice quickly from an accountant, or perhaps from Citizens' Information or MABS (the Money Advice and Budgeting Service).

Mortgage

A mortgage can be cleared on your death by a life policy. This means that your spouse or children, or whoever you leave the house to, can take the house mortgage-free.

If you don't have a life policy, unfortunately your beneficiary will have to take over the mortgage or sell the asset to clear it off. Check with the bank, building society or other financial institution with which you have your loan or mortgage.

Car Loan

A car loan will typically be either a loan or a hire purchase arrangement. With a loan, you own the car and you repay the bank. With a hire purchase agreement or finance deal, the car remains the property of the finance company until you have repaid the full amount of the debt.

Overdraft

A bank overdraft can be a useful facility for managing cash flow without having to borrow in the long term. Many people live their daily lives in the red. Check the interest rate and the amount of interest you are paying.

Credit Cards

If you pay the balance off in full and on time each month a credit card can be very useful, and a good way to make purchases. However, more than half of us don't pay it off each month, and so it becomes a niggling debt which can get out of hand quite quickly. Unfortunately, credit card debt does not die with you; if there is a balance remaining, it will have to be paid from your estate. Interest rates on credit cards are usually very high.

Total

Add it all up. You're probably worth more than you thought, even after you take out the mortgage and the other debts. Have the personal affairs and possessions list done before you go to see your solicitor about your will. It will help both you and the solicitor.

Note

Remember to record where important original documents, policies and deeds can be found, both for your wealth, succession and inheritance planning and in the event of your death.

Check the wording on your deeds for burdens and special conditions. Burdens include debts. These may be debts due by you or by a previous owner of your house or land. They may even be written on your deeds by mistake, for example because of a similarity between names. To remove burdens of debt due by you, you will have to pay to have them removed from your deeds.

My Personal Affairs
and Possessions List

The following is a checklist which, regardless of your age, you should complete, sign, date and give to your solicitor. Keep a copy in a safe place for your own records, and update it annually.

This checklist will be a vital source of information in the event of you becoming incapacitated and your representatives having to manage your affairs.

Emergencies

For emergencies, please contact my next of kin (husband, wife, partner, aunt, uncle, brother, sister, nephew, niece, cousin and so on), friend or neighbour, as follows:

Full name: . . . .
Telephone: . . . .
Mobile: . . . .
Home address: . . . .
Business address: . . . .
Email: . . . .

Full name: . . . .
Telephone: . . . .
Mobile: . . . .
Home Address: . . . .
Business Address: . . . .
Email: . . . .

Full name: . . . .
Telephone: . . . .
Mobile: . . . .
Home address: . . . .
Business address: . . . .
Email: . . . .

Medical

DOCTOR

Full name: . . . .
Telephone: . . . .
Mobile: . . . .
Home address: . . . .
Business address: . . . .
Email: . . . .

My blood type is: . . . .

DENTIST

Full name: . . . .
Telephone: . . . .
Mobile: . . . .
Home address: . . . .
Business address: . . . .
Email: . . . .

PSYCHIATRIST

Full name: . . . .
Telephone: . . . .
Mobile: . . . .
Home address: . . . .
Business address: . . . .
Email: . . . .

COUNSELLOR

Full name: . . . .
Telephone: . . . .
Mobile: . . . .
Home address: . . . .
Business address: . . . .
Email: . . . .

Legal

My PPS number/Pension number is: . . . .

SOLICITOR

Full name: . . . .
Firm: . . . .
Telephone: . . . .

Mobile: . . . .
Home address: . . . .
Business address: . . . .
Email: . . . .

EXECUTOR 1 (LEGAL PERSONAL REPRESENTATIVE)

Full name: . . . .
Telephone: . . . .
Mobile: . . . .
Home address: . . . .
Business address: . . . .
Email: . . . .

EXECUTOR 2

Full name: . . . .
Telephone: . . . .
Mobile: . . . .
Home address: . . . .
Business address: . . . .
Email: . . . .

ATTORNEY 1 (FOR ENDURING POWER OF ATTORNEY)

Full name: . . . .
Telephone: . . . .
Mobile: . . . .
Home address: . . . .
Business address: . . . .
Email: . . . .

ATTORNEY 2 (FOR ENDURING POWER OF ATTORNEY)

Full name: . . . .
Telephone: . . . .
Mobile: . . . .

Home address: . . . .
Business address: . . . .
Email: . . . .

ACCOUNTANT

Full name: . . . .
Firm: . . . .
Telephone: . . . .
Mobile: . . . .
Home address: . . . .
Business address: . . . .
Email: . . . .

FINANCIAL ADVISER

Full name: . . . .
Firm: . . . .
Telephone: . . . .
Mobile: . . . .
Home address: . . . .
Business address: . . . .
Email: . . . .

Funeral Arrangements

FUNERAL DIRECTORS/UNDERTAKERS:

Full name: . . . .
Firm: . . . .
Telephone: . . . .
Mobile: . . . .
Home address: . . . .
Business address: . . . .
Email: . . . .

My grave is at: . . . .

My mortal remains are to be interred at: . . . .

My mortal remains are to be cremated and then interred/spread at: . . . .

My funeral-arrangements document is located at: . . . .

My will is stored with:

Full name: . . . .
Firm: . . . .
Telephone: . . . .
Mobile: . . . .
Home address: . . . .
Business address: . . . .
Email: . . . .

My will was last uppdated on [day/month/year]: . . . .

My organs are to be donated to:

Full name: . . . .
Telephone: . . . .
Mobile: . . . .
Business address: . . . .
Email: . . . .

(Remember to make arrangements for the donation of your organs and always to carry your donor card.)

My body is to be donated for anatomical research to:

Research institution/University/
   Medical School: . . . .
Address: . . . .
Telephone: . . . .
Email: . . . .

Miscellaneous

People here and overseas to be notifed by my executors of my death:

Full name: . . . .
Telephone: . . . .
Mobile: . . . .
Home address: . . . .
Business address: . . . .
Email: . . . .

Full name: . . . .
Telephone: . . . .
Mobile: . . . .
Home address: . . . .
Business address: . . . .
Email: . . . .

The deeds of the property (or properties) are held by: . . . .
at: . . . .

My documents safe is located at: . . . .

MISCELLANEOUS CODES

For premises doors: . . . .
For computers: . . . .
For storage units: . . . .

KEYS

Home keys located at: . . . .
Business/premises keys located at: . . . .
Car keys located at: . . . .

Financial

EMPLOYERS

Full name: . . . .
Firm: . . . .
Telephone: . . . .
Mobile: . . . .
Home address: . . . .
Business address: . . . .
Email: . . . .

BANK (OR BANKS)

Full name: . . . .
Telephone: . . . .
Mobile: . . . .
Business address: . . . .
Email: . . . .

Bank account numbers: . . . .
. . . .

CREDIT CARD PROVIDER

Full name: . . . .
Telephone: . . . .
Mobile: . . . .
Business address: . . . .
Email: . . . .

Credit card numbers: . . . .

MORTGAGE PROVIDER/BROKER

Full name: . . . .
Telephone: . . . .
Mobile: . . . .
Business address: . . . .
Email: . . . .

Mortgage account numbers: . . . .

ACCOUNTANT

Full name: . . . .
Telephone: . . . .
Mobile: . . . .
Home address: . . . .
Business address: . . . .
Email: . . . .

FINANCIAL ADVISER

Full name: . . . .
Telephone: . . . .
Mobile: . . . .
Home address: . . . .
Business address: . . . .
Email: . . . .

INSURANCE

BUILDING INSURER

Full name: . . . .
Telephone: . . . .
Mobile: . . . .
Business address: . . . .
Email: . . . .
Policy number: . . . .

CONTENTS INSURER

Full name: . . . .
Telephone: . . . .
Mobile: . . . .
Business address: . . . .
Email: . . . .
Policy number: . . . .

CAR INSURER

Full name: . . . .
Telephone: . . . .
Mobile: . . . .
Business address: . . . .
Email: . . . .
Policy number: . . . .

ASSURANCE

INSURER

Full name: . . . .
Telephone: . . . .
Business address: . . . .
Email: . . . .
Policy number: . . . .

Pension

PENSION FUND PROVIDER

Full name: . . . .
Telephone: . . . .
Business address: . . . .
Email: . . . .

Pension fund policy number: . . . .

Company Directorships

Name of company: . . . .
Name of principal: . . . .
Telephone: . . . .
Mobile: . . . .
Home address: . . . .
Business address: . . . .
Email: . . . .

Estate and Asset List

State where located, giving addresses, folio numbers
(which relate to the plots of land you own): . . . .
House: . . . .
Land: . . . .
Investment property (management company, letting
    agent, and so on): . . . .
Interest in expectancy: . . . .
Bank/building society current/deposit/savings
accounts: . . . .
Credit Union: . . . .
Post Office: . . . .
Prize Bonds: . . . .

Cars, boats, motorcycles: . . . .
Stocks, shares, gold: . . . .
Pensions: . . . .
Life insurance/assurance: . . . .
Antiques, art, wine, heirlooms: . . . .
Jewellery: . . . .
Cash: . . . .

Religious

My preferred clergy are: . . . .
of . . . . church

Social and Professional

MEMBERSHIPS OF ORGANISATIONS/ASSOCIATIONS

Name(s) and address(es) of organisations/
associations: . . . .

MEMBERSHIPS OF PROFESSIONAL BODIES

Name(s) and address (es) of professional
bodies: . . . .

*

Note

Some accountants attempt to 'make' your will. Usually
they do not have either the legal training or the insurance cover to do so, so beware. Would you ask a dentist
to service your car?

7

Roles and Powers of Executors

Your executors ensure that, after your death, your property or estate passes to your chosen beneficiaries. When talking about executors, lawyers often use the term 'legal personal representative' (LPR or 'per rep').

You need only one executor but we recommend that you appoint two. The Probate Office of the High Court will accept a maximum of three. More than three requires Probate Office approval.

Put simply, the duty or role of the executor/personal representative is to:

(a) ascertain and gather all the assets

(b) ensure that all necessary assets are 'returned' to the Revenue Commissioners and that all taxes are paid

(c) take care of all the paperwork concerning the administration or probate, and then

(d) distribute the assets of the estate in accordance with both law and the directions given in the will.

It is useful to choose as an executor someone who is younger than you and has a good business brain. This is not essential, however, as executors can hire account-ants, solicitors and other qualified advisers to assist.

You can appoint a beneficiary as an executor. For a husband and wife who are both making wills, it is usual (but not always the case) for each to appoint the other as sole executor and beneficiary.

At the moment of your death, your executor's job be-gins.

Mortal Remains (the Body)

Believe it or not, the first duty of the executor(s) is to lay the testator's mortal remains to rest.

The executor, not the family, has custody of the re-mains until burial or cremation. On the death of a testa-tor, the executor should immediately look for and read the will. If the will states cremation of the remains, and instead the remains are interred without cremation, the terms of the will have not been carried out.

Such instructions may or may not be part of the will. Solicitors keep notes accompanying the will either in the testator's files or, more usually, in a special safe for wills, and these notes may instruct on the form of disposal of the remains after death. If there are such directions, it is important that the executors know about them.

Executor's Powers

Executors have various powers and a number of respon-sibilities under these powers. In addition to powers given under statue law (e.g. the Succession Act 1965), certain other powers may be given in your will.

Powers given to executors under the Succession Act 1965 include:

Power to sell

Your executors may sell all or part of your estate when you die in order to realise assets and pay debts, pay beneficiaries, and so on.

Power to act as trustees

You may appoint your executors as trustees in your will in order to make provision for your family.

Power to appropriate (Section 55)

Your executors can appropriate all or any part of your estate to satisfy the share of beneficiaries in the estate.

Power to appropriate the family home (Section 56)

Your executors can appropriate the family home in favour of a surviving spouse.

Power to lease (Section 60)
Power to mortgage (Section 60.3)

Your executors may raise money by way of mortgage or charge for the payment of expenses, debts and liabilities and legal right for the surviving spouse.

Power to compromise (Section 60.8)

Your executors can settle claims and disputes concerning the estate.

Your executor may also, with the approval of the beneficiaries or the court, raise money for the construction, repair, improvement or completion of buildings or for the improvement of land forming part of your estate when you die.

Conflict of Interest

This arises where a person involved in an estate has competing interests. Generally, a person who is appointed as an executor and a beneficiary under a will wouldn't normally have competing interests. They would have two roles to play – one as executor, the other as beneficiary – but as long as those roles are separated, there won't be a problem. However, when, for example, the executor tries either to make a profit for himself from his position as executor or perhaps decides to sue the estate, he would find himself in a conflict situation.

If a testatrix made a will appointing her son as executor but leaving all her worldly wares to charity, the son might, understandably, feel a little aggrieved. If he decides to sue his mother's estate for a share, he must resign as an executor, because he cannot sue himself. Anyone who takes action against an estate in which they are an executor must immediately resign as executor.

Conflicts regularly arise but, with foresight and careful planning, they can be avoided. Be careful who you choose as executor and try to imagine, first, whether they are honest enough to administer your estate (i.e. that they won't try to enrich themselves from the position) and second, whether they are likely to sue your estate when you're gone. Remember, spouses, ex-spouses and children are the main persons likely to sue your estate. If you take care of them while you're alive, to the best of your ability and in accordance with your means, they may not be able to sue, but if you don't, there is a risk. That is not to say that you shouldn't appoint your spouse as executor/executrix: in most cases, the spouse or one of the children is the logical choice.

Case study

For example, Jack and his wife Susan are in their seventies and have no children, but their niece Cathy has lived with them for years. They both regard Cathy as if she was their child.

Jack is the owner of the property, a house, and he decides to leave it to his wife Susan for her life and then to Cathy. He appoints Susan as executrix. Following Jack's death, other members of the extended family (on Susan's side of the family) influence Susan to claim her 'legal-right share' (half of the estate). Susan is 'entitled in law' to do so. She had not intended to do so, however, and was perfectly happy with a life interest, but she cooperates with her 'influencers' and claims half of the estate.

Cathy therefore will inherit only half of the estate and not the full estate – as Jack wished her to have after Susan's death. Susan now has a conflict of interest as she is claiming against the will that she is supposed to administer.

The net result may be that Cathy feels snubbed, and insists on the court appointing an independent executor. As a result, Susan feels snubbed. Cathy moves out and Susan finds herself estranged from the one person she thought would be caring for her and living with her for the rest of her days. A more detailed discussion when Jack was making his will might have avoided these problems.

In this example, the house, as the only substantial asset, may have to be sold, causing great disruption for Susan.

Think!

Here are some of the times in your life when you should consider updating your will:

- when you get married

- when you reach the age of eighteen

- when you inherit property

- when you separate or divorce

- when you buy property

- when you become a parent

- when you have a big win in the National Lottery

- when you retire from work.

8

Family, Friends and Relations

In most cases, your choice of executors and beneficiaries will be obvious. If not, then drawing up a list of your family members, extended family and friends will help you in deciding who your beneficiaries and executors may be.

Your family tree or genealogy can help decide ownership and entitlements, distinguish you from others of similar or the same names and, in cases of estates where probate or administration has not been taken out for generations help you clear up the estate and bring your affairs up to date.

This becomes especially relevant in situations of co-habitants/partners and where people die without making a will. A developed family tree will provide detail of kinship, bloodline and ancestors.

The usual starting point for developing a family tree is birth certificates, marriage certificates, death certificates, gravestones and church records. From these, it is usually possible to plot paternal and maternal lines of ancestry.

Genealogists, historians and local journalists may be of help to you in tracing your family tree.

9

The Tax Drivers

We don't know of any will that said: 'I leave 25 percent of my estate to the Revenue Commissioners.'

The tax you pay in life depends on your income or revenue. The tax that your beneficiaries will pay on receiving a benefit from you when you die will depend on their relationship to you and on the value of what you have left them. You may leave them a smaller tax bill if you plan ahead. When considering the terms of your will, it is always wise to explore how you can eliminate, or at least minimise, taxes for your chosen beneficiaries. Tax can be a major factor and can influence the decisions you make.

The categories of taxes that apply to inheritances are Capital Acquisitions Tax or CAT (which covers gifts and inheritances), Capital Gains Tax or CGT, Trust Tax and Probate Tax. CAT is generally the most important one to consider when dealing with the estate and so is the focus of our efforts here.

Don't Step Over the Thresholds

At the moment, the tax rate is 25 percent. The Indexed Group Thresholds for 2008 and 2009 (after indexation) are set out in the following table. As you will see, the taxes and thresholds have changed considerably over recent years, and they are likely to continue to change in the future.

RELATIONSHIP TO DONOR	GROUP THRESHOLDS		
	from prior to 20/11/08	from 20/11/08 to 7/4/09	from 8/4/09
GROUP A Son/ Daughter	€521,208	€542,544	€434,000
GROUP B Parent/ Brother/Sister/ Niece/Nephew/ Grandchild	€52,121	€54,254	€43,400
GROUP C Relationship other than Group A or B	€26,060	€27,127	€21,700

Plan Now, Save Later

Many people are not aware that by planning their will in the right way, their family and beneficiaries might save a significant value of the estate they will inherit. In fact, some may escape that tax altogether.

Think about it. You work hard all your life and pay your taxes. The last thing you want is your beneficiaries being hit with a sizeable tax bill after you are gone. The tax is likely to be paid from your estate, i.e. your assets.

For example, you leave your nephew €100,000 in cash. He has a threshold from you in 2009 of €43,400 and so he would pay tax on the remaining €56,600 at 25 percent, i.e. €14,150. You might think that this is only a small amount in the greater scheme of things, but that €14,150 comes from your money. The nephew will receive around €85,850 and would no doubt still be quite happy.

But what if you could save some of that €14,150? What if you left €50,000 each to two nephews? If you do this, total taxes will be €3,300, a saving of almost €11,000. By spreading your assets among your beneficiaries, you can legitimately reduce or eliminate tax liabilities, and the cash will end up with your beneficiaries rather than the Revenue Commissioners.

Relieved? You Should Be!

Certain reliefs are available from CAT, notably agricultural relief, business relief, favourite nephew/niece and dwelling house relief. While agricultural and business relief both have the effect of reducing values by 90 percent, favourite nephew/niece relief moves the nephew or niece from a Group B to a Group A threshold.

Dwelling house relief can be claimed by anyone who meets the criteria. If you qualify, the house that you are inheriting will be completely exempt from CAT. The advantage here is that the group threshold is not used up, so if you receive a house and some money, potentially only the money is taxable.

The Horse Has Bolted
But You Can Still Lock the Door

The best type of tax planning is done while you are alive and well. However, there is scope, in some cases, for what is known as 'Post-death tax planning'. This form of planning only arises where someone dies and the tax date has not yet been triggered. In many cases, the tax date will be the date the grant of probate is issued by the Probate Office. This can be six months or more from the date of death. It usually applies where a beneficiary is seeking a relief from tax, such as agricultural relief or business relief.

In seeking agricultural relief, it is necessary to look at the beneficiary's own assets to see if he passes the 'farmer test' and can avail of the relief.

To qualify, 80 percent or more of the beneficiary's assets, including the farm he is about to receive, must be agricultural in nature.

If he qualifies, he gets the relief, which reduces the value of the farm for tax purposes by 90 percent. If he does not qualify because of the value of his own assets, some or all of those assets can be transferred to his spouse.

This is essentially post-death tax planning. When the tax date arrives, he has little or no assets in his own name and so he will qualify for the relief. This type of planning can only be done where the beneficiary is married, as assets can only be transferred free of taxes where they are transferred to a spouse (as there is no tax between spouses).

How a Five-year Rule on Trusts
Can Cut Tax by 50 Percent

Ask your solicitor about the five-year rule on trusts. In making a will, people who have young children will often consider creating a discretionary trust. This is a trust where all property is left to the trustees appointed under the will; those trustees then hold the property until the children reach a certain age.

The testator determines the age at which the children get the property, but because it is a discretionary trust, the trustees decide on the division of the property between the children. This can give rise to discretionary trust tax (DTT) implications if the trust is not brought to an end before the youngest child reaches age twenty-one. When the youngest child reaches this age there is an initial tax liability of 6 percent and a further liability of 1 percent annually, until the trust is brought to an end.

If, however, the trust is brought to an end within five years of the youngest child's twenty-first birthday, a refund of 3 percent (i.e. half of the initial 6 percent charged) can be reclaimed. While discretionary trusts are a very useful way of providing for your children in the future, the tax hits can be avoided altogether by ending the trust before the youngest child reaches twenty-one.

CGT and Stamp Duty

As a general rule, CGT and Stamp Duty apply only to gifts; they do not apply to an inheritance. Therefore, if you receive a benefit from someone under their will, the only tax you really need to concern yourself with is CAT.

10

Wills for Different People

Your will may be similar to your brother's, sister's, friend's or neighbour's will. However, there will be distinct differences.

Your gold watch is unlikely to have exactly the same value as your friend's gold watch. Your family is unlikely to have exactly the same number of children, of the same age, as your neighbour. The property that you own will not be of the same value as that of your work colleague.

You may be single, married, separated, divorced, widowed, cohabiting, gay or lesbian. Your feelings, values, religion, goals, roles, wishes and intentions will be different from those of your own parents or siblings. Each case in Ireland and the world is different.

The following extracts from wills present different cases to give you a structure from which to develop your own ideas. Each has different legal and tax implications.

Read the clauses or conditions that you might include in your own will. Note them and consider them for discussion with your solicitor so that you will make a will that is best suited to your circumstances.

These extracts are for information only and should not be used as actual wills.

Married Person with Young Children Who Runs Own Business

This is the last will and testament of me John Cryan of Ballymore Manor, Glanmire, County Kildare, company director, and I hereby revoke all former wills and testamentary dispositions heretofore made by me.

Provided my wife Julia survives me by 30 days, then I leave, devise and bequeath my entire estate to her and appoint her as my sole executrix. I direct my wife to pay my just debts, funeral, etc. If my wife does not survive me by 30 days, then the following provisions shall apply:

I appoint . . . . of . . . . and . . . . of . . . . as my executors and trustees for the purpose of the Settled Land Acts 1882–90, the Conveyancing Acts 1882–92 and the Succession Act 1965 and I direct them to pay my just debts, funeral and testamentary expenses.

I appoint . . . . as testamentary guardians of my children.

I leave, devise and bequeath all my property to my trustees in trust for my children until the youngest reaches 18 and on reaching the age of 18 then in equal shares for their own use and benefit absolutely.

Another clause that is widely used is:

I leave my property to my trustees in trust for my children until the youngest reaches the age of 18 and then to one or more of my children in such share or shares as my trustees, in their absolute discretion, shall think fit.

Powers for Trustees

In addition to the powers conferred upon them by statute and by general law, I confer the following powers upon my executors and trustees:

A   The power to appoint new trustees under this my Will . . . .

B   The power on the realisation of any asset . . . .

C   To use the capital or income of my estate for the maintenance and/or improvement of any real property . . . .

D   To invest any asset forming part of my estate . . . .

To invest in unsecured interest-free loans to any beneficiary . . . .

To insure any asset . . . .

E   To pay the premiums out of the income or capital of my estate and

To use any monies paid on foot of such insurance policy to restore the asset . . . .

F   To carry on and continue any business I am engaged in . . . .

To use in the running of the said business . . . .

    To become employed in the said business . . . .

G   To borrow . . . .

H   To sell any asset . . . .

Unless any executor or trustee of this my will be proved to have acted dishonestly or wilfully committed a breach of trust, none of my executors or trustees shall be liable for any loss . . . .

Date: . . . .
Testator's signature: . . . .
Attestation clause (witnessing clause): . . . .
Witnesses' signatures: . . . .

Explanation

This is a typical will for a married person with young (minor) children. The first paragraph is the same for all wills: you must identify who is making the will and their address. Any other names or nicknames should be mentioned, as should any other recent previous addresses. The clause must also revoke any previous wills that may have been made.

The second paragraph is obvious: 'I leave everything to my wife'. The thirty-day requirement is inserted to ensure that the spouse, who in this example is also the beneficiary, survives long enough to inherit the estate. If the spouse survives for the required thirty days, they are entitled to receive the property comprised in the estate. If the spouse does not survive for thirty days, the alternative provisions in the will are activated.

An executor is required in every will; their role is to ensure that the assets pass to the chosen beneficiaries. The executor and beneficiary can of course be the same person (as in this case). The clause also includes an instruction for the executor (the spouse) to pay the funeral and other expenses and debts.

If the spouse (the wife, in this example) predeceases or dies within thirty days of her husband, the alternative executors become involved. In this sample will, the executors are also appointed as trustees. You can appoint your executors as trustees or you can choose two other people to be trustees if you wish. Trustees are important here because a trust has been set up for the benefit of the young children, as they are not old enough to receive property or assets, and so the trustees are given a legal power to manage assets for the benefit of the children.

Most wills contain alternative provisions in the event that a beneficiary either dies before the testator or does not survive the thirty days.

Guardians are also appointed. Your brother or sister (the uncle or aunt of your children) could be appointed. Typically, you might like to appoint the person or persons that the children like or know best. Imagine the people who would be 'first on the scene' with your children in the event of your sudden demise: the people you think of first are likely to be the guardians of your children in your will.

There are two possible scenarios as to how the trust property is to pass to the beneficiaries when they are old enough. The first is that the children will receive the property equally when the youngest child reaches a certain age. The second is where the splitting of the trust property is left to the discretion of the trustees. That might seem like a big decision for the trustees, but you have chosen them to deal with this, as you will not be there to do so.

When the trustees disperse the property to the children for tax purposes, it is as if the inheritance comes directly from the parent, and the usual parent/child tax threshold applies. The threshold is fixed at date of death.

If the property is not dispersed but is left in the trust after the youngest child/beneficiary reaches the age of twenty-one, a 6 percent discretionary trust tax is levied on the assets in the trust, plus 1 percent per annum thereafter.

Sometimes, people prefer to leave the assets locked in a trust until children are older than eighteen or twenty-one, or even over twenty-five, if they have concerns about assets being dissipated through immaturity or, possibly, addiction.

In relation to the last clause, if your executors/trustees do their best, with suitable advice when needed, they won't have any personal liability if things go wrong.

A Business/Farm Couple with Adult Children and One Clearly Identified Successor

This is the last will and testament of me Michael Murphy of Ballyfurlong, Miletown, County Galway, farmer, and I hereby revoke all former wills and testamentary dispositions heretofore made by me.

I appoint my wife Mary and my son Martin as executors of this my will and I direct them to pay my just debts, funeral and testamentary expenses.

I leave, devise and bequeath the house known as 'The Far House' and the contents therein and my adjacent 20 acres at Ballyfurlong to my wife Mary for her own use and benefit absolutely. It is my wish, though I am aware that my wish is not binding, that the said house and 20 acres will, following my wife's death, become the property of my son Martin.

I leave, devise and bequeath a site comprising one acre to each of my children John and Imelda together with the sum of €10,000 (ten thousand euro) each for their own use and benefit absolutely. The sites are to be taken from my lands at Knockmaroon but in any event they shall be chosen by agreement with my son Martin and should be those best suited to planning permission. In default of agreement as to the location of the sites, the decision of auctioneer Paddy Murphy shall be final and binding.

I leave, devise and bequeath the remainder of my lands at Knockmaroon, comprising 120 acres approximately, together with a dwelling house thereon known as 'The Near House', the contents therein and all stock, machinery and entitlements thereon, to my son Martin for his own use and benefit absolutely.

I leave, devise and bequeath all the rest residue and remainder of my property, including all financial assets, to my wife Mary for her own use and benefit absolutely.

Date: . . . .
Testator's signature: . . . .
Attestation clause (witnessing clause): . . . .
Witnesses' signatures: . . . .

Explanation

This type of will can be used equally well and is easily adapted to any kind of business. You need to describe accurately the property and assets that the business comprises so that the correct assets pass to the correct beneficiaries.

Here, the testator has appointed his wife and one of his sons as executors. While only one executor is needed, it is always better to have two, in case one decides not to act, cannot act, becomes incapacitated, or dies.

There are two houses in this example. Michael and Mary live in one and Martin lives in the other. It is vital to describe the houses appropriately. While it will be obvious to the family as to who lives in each house, the structuring of the will requires that the houses and lands passing to the beneficiaries must be accurately described in order to avoid ambiguity or confusion. The acreage and location of the lands, are both given. It is better to overdescribe rather than underdescribe property in order to provide clarity in the will.

There is a wish expressed in this will: that the house and twenty acres will go to Martin after Mary's death. If

Michael dies and Mary gets the property, she is free to do with it as she pleases. There is no obligation on Mary to leave the house and lands to Martin. Michael could have left her the property for her lifetime, with the property then passing to Martin on Mary's death, but in this example he is providing greater security for his wife.

A site and money have been left to the two other children. Obviously, Michael has only one farm, and so he cannot leave it to them all. Nor can he split it between them, as it would then probably cease to be a viable business. If we were talking about a large family business, one in which all three children had a desire to work, then it could perhaps make sense to give it to all three children equally. If this were done, then it may be necessary to have the three children make some sort of payment – an annual or lump sum – in favour of his wife, to provide adequate financial security for her into the future.

When it comes to bequests of money in a will, the safest option is always to use both words and figures, as you would when writing a cheque. As far greater care goes into the writing of the words, it is generally accepted that if there is a discrepancy between the words and figures, the words will be followed.

One other point worth mentioning in relation to the sites and money payment to John and Imelda is Section 117 of the Succession Act. Michael's motivation for leaving them such benefits under his will is no doubt driven by a desire to treat all children with some degree of equality, but it also helps guard his estate from challenge from John or Imelda.

The residue is left to Mary. This includes any monies in the bank, credit union and so on. Again, Michael Murphy's motivation for doing this is clearly to provide adequate financial security for his wife.

Married Person, Urban Situation, Single House

This is the last will and testament of me Jennifer Short of 5 Alta Villas, Urbanstown, Dublin 12, and I hereby revoke all former wills and testamentary dispositions heretofore made by me.

Provided my husband Tom survives me by 30 days, I give, devise and bequeath the whole of my estate to him and I appoint him my sole executor. If my husband does not survive me by thirty days, the following provisions shall apply:

I appoint my son Brian and daughter Mary as executors of this my will and I direct them to pay my just debts, funeral and testamentary expenses.

I direct my executors to sell my property and to divide the proceeds thereof in five equal shares between my children, Brian, Mary, Maurice, Peter and Lisa.

Date: . . . .
Testator's signature: . . . .
Attestation clause (witnessing clause): . . . .
Witnesses' signatures: . . . .

Explanation

This type of will is usually done by a married couple. Each spouse of course makes a will, and they are often called 'mirror wills', as the contents of one are reflected in the other.

Here, Jennifer has left her entire estate to her husband Tom – provided that he survives her by thirty days – and she has appointed him as sole executor. The thirty-day clause is a legal requirement. It is usually inserted into this type of will as there has to be a definite period of survival for the other spouse to inherit the estate. If the other spouse dies within the thirty days, the other provisions in the will are activated. In 90 percent of cases, the surviving spouse would not go to see the solicitor within the thirty-day period.

If the spouses die together, in circumstances where it is impossible to determine who died first (for example, a plane crash), they are deemed to have died simultaneously. In most other cases, it will be clear who died first. In any event, if both spouses die within the thirty-day period, the other provisions in the will become relevant.

In this example, Jennifer has five children, two of whom have been appointed as executors. Sometimes people will appoint the oldest children as executors. Here, the executors are instructed to sell the house and to divide the proceeds between all five children. Depending on market conditions, it may be difficult to sell the house. If this were to happen, the executors, by agreement with the beneficiaries, could rent the property in the short term, until the market improves. Remember, the 'proceeds' are what is left after the payment of debts and liabilities on the property. This could include a mortgage or legal and estate agents' fees.

This will is balanced and fair, and no child could feel hard done by in this example. Parents are usually motivated to provide for all children equally so as not to offend or upset any of the children, or where all children are doing equally well in life.

A Widow with One Down's Syndrome Child and Other Children

This is the last will and testament of me Sarah Denning of High Street, Enniscorthy, County Wexford, and I hereby revoke all former wills and testamentary dispositions heretofore made by me.

I appoint my daughters Rosemary and Sinead to be my executrices and trustees of this my will and I appoint them as trustees for the purposes of the Settled Land Acts 1882–90 and the Conveyancing Acts 1881–92 and the Succession Act 1965 and I direct them to pay my just debts, funeral and testamentary expenses. I also appoint my said daughters Rosemary and Sinead as guardians of my daughter Marguerite should guardianship be necessary.

I leave the sum of €5,000 (five thousand euro) to Mary Nolan of 2 Willow Heights, Enniscorthy, County Wexford, who has been such a good friend to me over so many years.

I leave the sum of €5,000 (five thousand euro) to the Parish Priest for the time being of St Aidan's Diocese for masses at a reasonable stipend per mass for the repose of my soul and the souls of my deceased husband Jim and his and my relatives and friends.

I give, devise and bequeath all the rest residue and remainder of my property as to one half thereof to my said daughters Rosemary and Sinead in equal shares share and share alike for their own use and benefit absolutely and the other half thereof I leave to my Trustees to hold in Trust for my said daughter Marguerite for her lifetime and to use same for Marguerite's benefit as my Trustees think fit for matters reasonably needed by Marguerite which are not met by any State or other benefits to which she is entitled and being received by her.

Following Marguerite's death, all funds remaining in the Trust to be divided equally between my said daughters Rosemary and Sinead absolutely. Should either of the said daughters have predeceased me or Marguerite, as applicable, leaving a child or children, then the share of the predeceased daughter shall be divided between the children of the said predeceased daughter in equal shares, share and share alike.

Or, alternative clause (to replace the paragraph above): Following Marguerite's death, I direct my Trustees to give all funds remaining in the said Trust to the County Wexford Community Workshop (Enniscorthy) Ltd for use for its charitable purposes, entirely at the discretion of its board of directors.

Powers for trustees can be added, as in the will for the married person with young children (see page 62).

Dated, signed, etc.

Explanation

In this will, the testatrix is widowed and has three children. She is trying to make reasonable provision for each of her children but would obviously like to leave a larger portion of her estate to Marguerite, who might need it most. Typically, parents in this situation will divert a larger sum towards a child with a disability, and in almost all cases the other children would not object.

Rosemary and Sinead are the clear choice as executrices. Time may be crucial here, depending on Marguerite's financial and other needs, and Rosemary and Sinead can deal with the assets and start administering the estate as soon as possible. Rosemary and Sinead are also appointed as trustees and guardians for Marguerite.

There are initial monetary bequests (sometimes also called pecuniary legacies) to Sarah's old friend Mary Nolan and to the parish priest for masses to be said. Words and figures are used here also. Given the size of the bequest to Mary, she shouldn't have any tax to pay, but much would depend on whether Mary had received any prior gifts or inheritances which could be added to this one. The priest is receiving €5,000 for masses. This type of bequest is considered to be charitable in nature and therefore not taxable.

Rosemary and Sinead have also been left half of the residue of the estate equally between them. To say 'one quarter to Rosemary and one quarter to Sinead' would have the same effect. Marguerite will receive the other half, but this is to be placed in trust for her because she is unable to manage the money herself. The trustees can be given as many powers in the will as may be required to enable them to manage the trust fund and to release or pay money out for Marguerite as she needs it. Marguerite may be on a disability pension but there is a risk that the pension may be reduced by the State or stopped altogether. In cases like this, the State (the Department of Social and Family Affairs) carries out a means test on Marguerite to assess her level of income. The purpose of this exercise is to determine whether the amount of money she receives from her mother's estate is enough to warrant a reduction in her pension. If payments are made out of the trust on an irregular basis, the pension should not be affected. There are no tax implications on trust funds for the incapacitated child.

If Marguerite dies but there is still some money in the trust, that money will pass to Rosemary and Sinead. There is a further provision in this will in favour of Rosemary and Sinead's children. If either of them died, their share of the estate will be divided equally between their children. In some cases, where the disabled child has been attending a special school or other institution, the parent may wish to leave any balance remaining after the child's death to that school or institution as a gesture of thanks.

At the moment, there is an issue as to whether the appointment of guardians for a person over eighteen is valid in law. This is on the basis that the person is of full age. However, it is always safer to appoint guardians when dealing with an incapacitated child, irrespective of their age.

Think!

Living Will Confusion

Many people assume that they can provide for their care in the future through making an Advance Care Directive, also known popularly as a 'Living Will'. Although the situation may change in the future, there is at present no legislation in Ireland for Advance Care Directives. On the other hand, such a directive may be valid. Whether it is enforceable is debatable. If you are concerned about provision for your care, you should ask your solicitor, who may advise that you make an Enduring Power of Attorney (EPA).

A Same-sex Couple

This is the last will and testament of me Michelle Murphy of 96 Hillside, Milltown, Galway, and I hereby revoke all former wills and testamentary dispositions heretofore made by me.

I appoint my partner Sarah Smith as executrix of this my will and I direct her to pay my just debts, funeral and testamentary expenses.

I leave, devise and bequeath my dwelling known as 96 Hillside, together with the contents therein, to the said Sarah Smith for her own use and benefit absolutely.

I leave the proceeds of my 'Section 60' policy to be used in the first instance to discharge any Capital Acquisitions Tax due on any inheritance by my partner Sarah Smith under my will and the remainder thereof to be used to discharge proportionately any Capital Acquisitions Tax due on any benefits received hereunder by my brothers and sisters and the balance thereof to form part of my residue.

All the rest residue and remainder of my property I leave to be divided in six equal shares between my five brothers and sisters Kathleen, Mary, Sean, Liam and Michael and my partner Sarah Smith in equal shares share and share alike.

Dated, signed, etc.

Explanation

Here we assume that the apartment is in Michelle's sole name. The apartment has been left to Sarah, so this, at least, provides Sarah with the security of having a roof over her head.

Tax-wise, as Michelle and Sarah live together, Michelle should be able to avail of dwelling house relief. This is a full exemption from CAT. Sarah's tax threshold is only €21,700, so the relief here is crucial. However, in this case Michelle has taken out a Section 60 policy (now a Section 72 policy) to cover any potential taxes that might arise. This policy covers taxes for all beneficiaries.

The residue would include any money in the bank, her car, Prize Bonds, shares, and so on. This would be divided six ways, and Sarah is therefore 'spreading' the money around between her beneficiaries to make full use of their available thresholds.

What would have happened if Michelle had left the house to the Cats and Dogs Home? As Michelle and Sarah are not married, Sarah has no Succession Act rights in Michelle's estate. Michelle is free to leave her house to whoever she wishes, and sadly Sarah could do nothing about it. It is hoped that the law in this area will be changed soon to provide unmarried couples with all the tax and legal rights that are presently available to married persons.

Think!

How do you decide who should be your witnesses?

- Persons who will *not* benefit from your will

- Must be over eighteen

- Must be of sound mind

- Must be able to see.

A Brother and Sister Living Together

The following wills assume that the sister is the sole owner of the dwelling house where they live.

Brother's Will

This is the last will and testament of me John Roche of 53 Rafter Heights, Strokestown, County Roscommon, and I hereby revoke all former wills and testamentary dispositions heretofore made by me.

I appoint my nephews Mark and Michael, sons of my late brother Peter, as my executors and I direct them to pay my just debts, funeral and testamentary expenses.

I leave all my estate, right title or interest in the property known as 53 Rafter Heights, Strokestown, County Roscommon, and the contents thereof to my nephew Mark for his own use and benefit absolutely.

I leave my shares in CRH and Kerry Group plc to my nephew Michael absolutely.

I leave my two brood mares and any other bloodstock to my good friend Brendan Shaughnessy and I hope he will have some luck with them.

I leave my fishing rods and all my fishing gear to my grandnephew Arthur and I wish him many years of 'tight lines'.

I leave all my woodworking equipment including the lathe and router to the Strokestown Community Workshop to assist them in their woodworking enterprise, but should they not require same, my executors shall sell same on the best available terms, and the proceeds thereof shall form part of the residue of my estate.

All the rest residue and remainder of my estate I leave as to 50 percent thereof to my sister Mary and 25 percent thereof each to my said nephews and executors Mark and Michael.

Dated, signed, etc.

Explanation

Here, Mark and Michael are described as nephews and so it is important to show whether they are nephews by blood or by marriage. This is very important when it comes to dealing with them in their capacity as beneficiaries. Blood nephews have a tax threshold of €43,400 in 2009 but nephews related by marriage have a tax threshold of only €21,700 in 2009.

John has left whatever interest he owns in the house to Mark. However, the house actually belongs to Mary. Therefore, all John really has to leave to Mark are the contents of the house. This could disappoint Mark, but nothing can be done about it.

However, when you look at Mary's will (below), she has left her house to John. If Mary dies first, John will get the house; John has covered this eventuality in his will.

The shares are left to Michael. Provided John has not disposed of the shares during his lifetime, or the company in which the shares are held has not changed status, he will receive the shares on John's death.

The mares, bloodstock, fishing rods and gear are all straightforward bequests.

The woodworking equipment has been left, in the first instance, to the workshop, but if they do not want it (possibly due to poor condition), then it can be sold, and the money received will form part of the residue.

Fifty percent of the residue is left to Mary, with the other 50 percent being divided between Mark and Michael equally.

Mary, Mark and Michael all fall into Group B threshold and can each inherit €43,400 in 2009 before incurring any tax liability. The value of the assets will determine whether they will have to pay any tax.

Sister's Will

This is the last will and testament of me Mary Roche of 53 Rafter Heights, Strokestown, County Roscommon, and I hereby revoke all former wills and testamentary dispositions heretofore made by me.

I appoint my nephews Mark and Michael as my executors and I direct them to pay my just debts, funeral and testamentary expenses.

I leave such car as I may have at the date of my death to my niece Pauline for her own use and benefit absolutely.

I confirm that I have nominated my account at Strokestown Credit Union to my niece Amanda for her own use and benefit absolutely.

I leave the proceeds of my deposit account at Bank of Ireland Strokestown to my niece Lucy for her own use and benefit absolutely.

I leave my dwelling house known as 53 Rafter Heights, Strokestown, County Roscommon, to my brother John for his own use and benefit absolutely but should he predecease me I direct my executors to sell same and I direct that the proceeds thereof shall form part of my residue.

All the rest residue and remainder of my estate I leave to be divided as follows: 5 percent to . . . . ,

10 percent to . . . . , 15 percent to . . . . , 20 percent to . . . . , 25 percent to . . . . , 25 percent to . . . .

Dated, signed, etc.

Explanation

Mary owns the house, so it will form part of her estate when she dies.

Regarding the car, no specific make or model is given; this is always preferable in a will. If a specific make or model is mentioned, e.g. a VW Golf, but Mary changed her car to a Ford Fiesta before she died, then Pauline would not get the car. Classic cars of course must be mentioned specifically.

The Credit Union account is already nominated to Amanda. Therefore, she gets the proceeds of that account outside the terms of the will. As such, it doesn't really need to be mentioned here at all, but it is in the will for the avoidance of doubt. It doesn't affect the validity of the will.

There is a danger with the deposit account. If Mary closes the account, transfers the money to another account or bank, or simply spends the money, then Lucy will get nothing. It would be better just to leave a specific sum of money to Lucy.

If John survives Mary, he will get the house. Contents are not mentioned, so unfortunately they will fall into the residue. John could always come to an agreement with the residuary beneficiaries, who most likely would not want the contents either way.

The residue is split into percentages. When doing this, it is vital to check and double-check that they add up to 100 percent. If it is under 100 percent, then there is a partial intestacy of the shortfall. If it is over 100 percent, then the benficiaries can try to come to some agreement on the split, or they can fight about it in court. It's cheaper to agree.

An Opposite-sex Cohabiting Couple with Young Children, House in Joint Names

This is the last will and testament of me Bridget Kennedy of Grove Park, Springfield, Cork, and I hereby revoke all former Wills and Testamentary Dispositions heretofore made by me.

I appoint my partner Sean Burke as executor of this my will and I direct him to pay all my just debts, funeral and testamentary expenses. I appoint Sean as guardian of my children.

I give, devise and bequeath all my estate of every nature and kind, wheresoever situate, both real and personal, to my partner Sean for his own use and benefit absolutely.

If my partner Sean predeceases me then I appoint my sister Joanne and her husband Mike as my executors and trustees (hereinafter called 'my trustees') for the purpose of the Settled Land Acts 1882–90, the Conveyancing Acts 1881–92 and The Succession Act 1965 and I direct them to pay my just debts, funeral and testamentary expenses.

I appoint my trustees as guardians of my children.

I leave the sum of €1,000 (one thousand Euros) each to my said sister Joanne and her husband Mike for their own use and benefit absolutely.

I give, devise and bequeath all the rest residue and remainder of my property to my trustees in trust for my children until the youngest child attains the age of 21 years then in equal shares for their own use and benefit absolutely.

Powers for trustees can be added, as in the will for the married person with young children (see page 62).

Dated, witnessed, etc.

Explanation

In this example, the couple are not married and both are the natural parents of the children. This will is similar to that of a married person with young children; however, there are a number of differences. First of all, cohabiting couples have no rights under the Succession Act to a share in their deceased partners' estate. In this example, as the entire estate has been left to the partner, it doesn't pose a problem from a legal perspective.

The house is held jointly between them. There are two ways people can hold property jointly: one as joint tenants, the other as tenants in common. If they own the house as joint tenants, then it will pass, outside the terms of the will, to the survivor, which is Sean. This is called 'survivorship'. So, even if Bridget didn't make a will, Sean would inherit her share of the house and so the whole ownership of the house will pass to Sean. If Sean and Bridget own the house as tenants in common, then the house will not pass to Sean automatically. Instead, Bridget's half of the property will pass in accordance with the terms of her will. In this case, there won't be any problem as Sean is entitled to the house under her will but if the estate was not left to Sean, it could cause huge difficulties for him. It is essential in all cases where property is owned jointly to check the deeds to see which form of joint ownership exists.

As Sean and Bridget are not married, Sean is not the automatic legal guardian of the children. In non-marital situations, only the mother is the automatic guardian. That may be hard to believe for all the fathers out there and it may seem unfair, but unfortunately that's the law. To get around that problem, Bridget could, during her lifetime, sign a declaration stating that she appoints Sean as the joint legal guardian of the children. Alternatively, she could apply to court seeking an order declaring Sean as joint legal guardian of the children. She has appointed Sean as guardian in her will, so this only becomes effective when she dies. Guardianship can be very important, particularly if there were domestic problems between Sean and Bridget before her death. Sean could end up in a battle for guardianship and custody of the children with Bridget's parents.

Sean is to receive all property under the will. This would include any bank accounts or other property held in Bridget's sole name. Depending on how much that is, this might result in tax implications for Sean. Irrespective of whether Sean receives property by survivorship or under the will, all benefits are potentially taxable. Sean is deemed to be a stranger in blood to Bridget, and so his tax threshold in 2009 is a mere €21,700. He would most likely qualify for a full tax exemption on the value of the half-share in the house passing to him. This is known as dwelling house relief. As it is a full exemption from tax, his threshold remains intact. He could inherit a further €21,700 before having to pay any tax. Above this, he will pay tax at 25 percent. Depending on what he is receiving, this could result in a sizeable tax bill. It is hoped that legislation will soon be enacted to provide cohabiting couples with similar legal and tax rights to those of married couples, where certain criteria are met. Most other European countries have already adopted similar legislation.

The rest of the will is quite straightforward in that alternative provisions are made in the event of Sean predeceasing Bridget. This includes the appointment of executors, trustees and guardians. In this case, all three 'hats' – executor, trustee and guardian – are being worn by Bridget's sister and her husband. This is not at all unusual.

The trust is set up for the trustees to hold the trust property until the youngest child reaches twenty-one, at which point it will be divided equally between all the children.

*

Please note that these sample wills are not complete documents. They are provided only to give you hints and tips as part of your preparation for visiting your solicitor. Some thoughts for other situations are given below.

A Single Person with No Children

The will for a single person with no children is similar to the Brother and Sister wills given on pages 77 and 79.

A Separated Person

Remember, you are still married and your spouse may have succession rights. Are there 'blocking' provisions in your separation agreement or court order?

A Divorced Person

Were succession rights 'blocked' in the divorce court order? Are you contemplating marriage? Children's inheritance rights remain. Review your will as soon as you get divorced, as your will is not revoked on divorce.

A Divorced Person Who Has Remarried

Check if the divorce order blocked succession rights for your former spouse. You cannot claim Succession Act rights against your former spouse's estate if you have remarried.

11

Challenging a Will

Up to the 1960s, the person making the will (the testator) was free to dispose of his property as he saw fit. We say 'he', as at that time assets were usually in the man's name. He could be as arbitrary and capricious in his will as he pleased. As long as he was mentally competent, the court would not intervene to 'change' his will, even if he left his family in a crisis.

The Succession Act

In the 1960s, the late Charles J. Haughey, then Minister for Justice, argued that the right to disinherit a spouse in a family was unacceptable and that there was no basis, moral or historical, for the view that it was acceptable.

He also argued that in the context of the Irish Constitution's view of the family, freedom of testation was an indefensible paradox. He said that it was emphasised by Article 41 of the Constitution, which recognises the support which a married woman gives to the State by her life within the home, without which the common good could not be achieved. He argued further that the State for its part must undertake to ensure that mothers should not be obliged by economic necessity to engage in labour to the neglect of duties in the home or towards their children.

The Succession Act, which came into effect in 1965, gives protection to a spouse and to children. It allows the surviving spouse to claim a fixed share of the deceased spouse's estate, even if the will tries to 'cut out' that spouse. The share is known as the legal-right share.

We now look at the spouse's position in two different situations, the first where there is a will, and the second where there is no will.

Spouse's Position Where There Is a Will

If there are no children, and the spouse is omitted from the will, the spouse is entitled to half of the estate.

If the spouse is omitted and there are children, the spouse is entitled to one third of the estate.

Spouse's Position Where There Is No Will

If there is no will and no children, the spouse inherits the entire estate.

If there is no will and there are children, the spouse inherits two-thirds of the estate and the children take the remaining one third between them.

Is the spouse obliged to take her share?

The spouse is not obliged or forced to do anything. There are many situations where a spouse is perfectly satisfied that the bulk of the estate is left, perhaps to one of the children, and the spouse might be satisfied with, say, a pension which is already in place, and a right of residence for life in the dwelling house. The point is that the 'spouse's legal right' is a protection which is built in for spouses. It is a legal right which they can call upon if they find themselves in a bad situation due to inadequate or capricious provisions in the will.

Spouse's Challenge to a Will

You can see from the above that a spouse can 'challenge' a will by calling for their legal-right share. While it is a protection that is properly built into our legislation, it is a situation which should be avoided if possible by careful and complete discussion at the time the will is being made. The reality, of course, is that all the advice in the world will not always deter someone from putting odd or unusual provisions into the will.

Children's Challenge to a Will

A child cannot challenge the will if the child's surviving parent (the surviving spouse) is the sole beneficiary in the will.

In other situations, however, because of the provisions of Section 117 of the Succession Act 1965, a child can challenge a will. The child could be successful in that challenge if he or she can prove to a court that the testator failed in his or her moral duty to make proper provision for that child having regard to all the circumstances, including the child's position in life, the situation of other beneficiaries, and the means or assets of the testator.

Such a challenge should not be undertaken without careful and experienced advice, as recent High Court cases have indicated that severe cost penalties could apply. Up to recently, it was generally thought that no matter what the outcome of a challenge to a will, all the legal costs would be paid out of the estate and the challenger thus had a 'free shot' at the will. Indications from recent cases, however, make it clear that there can be a serious cost risk to a badly founded challenge.

Time limit

If a child wishes to make such a claim, there is a strict six-month time limit from the date of the grant of probate.

Testator Was Mentally Incapable

It is a very serious challenge to make to a will that the testator was mentally incapable. There are occasions, particularly when wills are made at a time of serious illness, where someone in the family will allege, after the testator's death, that the testator was mentally incapable of making the will.

If that is proved to be correct, the court will strike the will down or make it null and void. Medical records and opinions will form a crucial part of such a case, but the final decision is a legal one, to be made by the judge hearing the case.

Undue Influence

A will could be struck down, or a benefit under it made null and void, if it can be proved that someone exerted undue influence on the testator at the time that he was making the will, for instance to make a devise or bequest in their favour.

Legal Costs

From the foregoing paragraphs, you can see that gathering all necessary facts and information about the testator, about possible 'mental incapacity' and possible 'undue influence', could involve a huge amount of time and cost. Costs on all sides in the ensuing court case could wipe out a large portion of the estate. It is vital to consider these situations calmly and carefully before embarking on such a challenge. If, however, there is a genuine case, the costs are usually paid from the estate.

As recently as 2008, the Irish Supreme Court allowed costs from an estate, reversing a High Court Order which made the challengers partly responsible for costs. The decision clearly shows, however, that challengers can be held personally responsible for costs, and so great care is needed when assessing such a challenge.

12

Securing a Will

Against Challenge

People often have good reason to ensure that a challenge to their will is discouraged. They may fear that the property that they have worked for will fall into the wrong hands if someone challenges their will. They may wish to discourage a family member or relation from incurring the cost of taking a case to court. They may wish to prevent a husband, wife or partner from being influenced into making costly mistakes.

Can a Testator 'Block' the Spouse's 'Legal Right Share'?

Yes, in some situations:

If, for example, at the time the will is being made there is complete consensus between the testator/testatrix and spouse

and

if it is clear that the spouse is satisfied with very minimal provisions being made (a life interest only) *and*

if the spouse makes it clear that he/she has no intention whatsoever of calling in the 'legal-right share',

then

it would be wise to have that spouse separately and independently advised (by a different solicitor) before signing a renunciation of succession rights document.

This prevents other family members, usually with ulterior motives, from influencing the surviving spouse.

Blocking Orders in Separation and Divorce Cases

'Blocking' succession rights can be agreed or ordered by the court.

When parties are separated, they are still husband and wife. Unless blocking orders are made at the time of the granting of the separation whereby neither spouse will have a right to inherit from the other's estate, the surviving spouse will inherit as if there was no separation at all.

Even in a divorce situation, where the parties are no longer husband and wife, the survivor will still have a right to make an application for a share of the estate, unless 'blocking' orders exist.

Preventing Children from Challenging a Will

The best protection against a challenge from children is to discuss carefully the position in life of each child with your solicitor. 'Children' in this context can often mean adults.

Ensure that the solicitor records your instructions and the reason for the decisions you are making in your will.

Where a child challenges your will, your solicitor would disclose very early in play those instructions to the solicitor for the challenger. The challenger's legal team would quickly become aware that there were very good and sensible reasons for the provisions in your will, and if so, that should be the end of the challenge. This procedure can put the challenger at risk of incurring legal costs.

13

When There's No Will: Intestacy

Your family could be thrown into uncertainty, chaos and trauma if you die without having made a will or if you have made an invalid will. Not having made a will, or having made an invalid will, means that you have died intestate.

Your family members will have the extremely difficult task of trying to cope with grief while at the same time dealing with the uncertainty and cost involved in unscrambling complex legal and financial matters of your estate, no matter how small.

The cost to them will be enormous, no matter how you look at it. That is the cost to them of you having died intestate. Your closest surviving next of kin will have to pick up the pieces. You may have left a legacy of family conflict, as well as costly court battles.

If you die intestate, the law will decide on the administration of your estate. The law will first have to decide who your closest next of kin is. Is your closest next of kin your spouse or is it a civil partner? Is it an uncle, an aunt or a cousin? The next 'decision' of the law will be to determine who is entitled to your estate. How much of your estate each family member can get depends on the relationship of your beneficiary to you, the testator/testatrix, and is given in the table below:

Relative Surviving	Distribution of Estate
Spouse and issue	Two-thirds to spouse; one third equally among children, with issue of pre-deceased child taking *per stirpes**
Spouse and no issue (i.e. no offspring)	Spouse takes all
Issue and no spouse	Children take equally, with children of a predeceased child taking *per stirpes**
Father, mother, brothers and sisters	Each parent takes one half
One parent, brothers and sisters	Parent takes all
Brothers and sisters	All take equally; children of a predeceased brother or sister take *per stirpes**
Nephews, nieces and grandparent	Nephews and nieces take all equally
Nephews, nieces, uncles, aunts and great-grandparents	Nephews and nieces take all equally
Uncles, aunts and great-grandparents	Uncles and aunts take all equally
First cousin, great uncle, great nephew and great-grandparent	First cousin, great uncle and great nephew take all equally

* Example of *per stirpes.* Father died some years ago. Mother died recently. She was survived by three children. But a fourth child predeceased her, leaving two children of his own. Three surviving children take one quarter each, and the children of the predeceased child take their parent's share between them.

Conclusion

If you have made a will, Congratulations. If you review your will every few years, and when your circumstances change, Congratulations again. If you have made no will, we urge you to make one. The benefits are many. By making your will, you may provide for children, for family, for relatives, for friends and for your favourite charity; reduce stress and trauma; reduce or perhaps avoid tax; avoid family feuds; prevent costly court cases; and keep the State from getting your property.

The process will give you clarity, and you may learn a great deal about what you owe, what you own and what you can do in both of these areas. Good advice yields good options, and good options yield solutions.

Making a will is a private matter. Solicitors sign an oath of confidentiality. So nobody is going to know anything about your will unless you tell them.

Making a will is inexpensive when compared to a lifetime of trauma and uncertainty. There is the satisfaction of knowing that, having made your will, you are leaving a good legacy. And there is the great consolation of knowing that your affairs are in order.

Recommended Reading

Padraic Courtney and others, *Wills, Probate and Estates*, Law Society of Ireland

Albert Keating, *Probate Law and Practice*

Joe Martin and Paul Reck, *Taxation Summary*

Eamonn Mongey, *Probate Practice in a Nutshell*

Alan Moore, *Tax Magic*

John G. Murphy and Jason Dunne, *Inheritance and Succession: The Complete Irish Guide*, and see *www.myinheritance.ie*

Brian Spierin, *Irish Will Precedents*

Citizens Information, see *www.citizensinformation.ie*

Revenue Commissioners, see *www.revenue.ie*

Succession Act 1965, see *www.irishstatutebook.ie*